The *Active Reader*

Book 2

Linda Kita-Bradley

Cobourg Campus
The Fleming Building, Top Floor
1005 Elgin Street West
Cobourg, ON K9A 5J4

Grass Roots Press

Edmonton, Alberta, Canada
2011

The Active Reader – Book 2 © 2011 Grass Roots Press

The Active Reader – Book 2 is published by

Grass Roots Press
A division of Literacy Services of Canada Ltd.
www.grassrootsbooks.net

AUTHOR	Linda Kita-Bradley
PASSAGES	Contributing Writer: Joyce Cameron
EDITOR	Pat Campbell
DESIGN	Lara Minja
LAYOUT	Susan Hunter
PILOTING	Vancouver Community College, Basic Education Department

ACKNOWLEDGEMENTS

We acknowledge the financial support of the Government of Canada through the Book Publishing Industry Development Program (BPIDP) for our publishing activities.

We acknowledge the support of the Alberta Foundation for the Arts for our publishing programs.

ISBN 978-1-926583-16-7

Printed in Canada

Contents

About this workbook

Welcome to Book 2 of *The Active Reader* series. This workbook aims to engage learners in the process of active reading by providing stimulating reading passages that help learners develop the skills and strategies to become fluent readers.

The workbook is organized around five themes: people, relationships, health and safety, the environment, and history. Each theme consists of two units that provide the following activities:

Pre-reading
Photos and discussion questions introduce the topic, activate learners' background knowledge, and provide a purpose for reading.

Main Reading Passage
Learners are encouraged to read a non-fiction passage with strategically placed "Stop and Think" questions. Sidebars explain vocabulary or provide additional information to enhance the readers' understanding.

Post-reading
Questions require students to recall factual information, make inferences, identify main idea, and make personal connections to the text.

Mini-Lesson
Learners focus on making inferences, finding main ideas, and recognizing the organization of text.

Literacy Practice
Learners are encouraged to engage in daily literacy practices through reading, analyzing, and discussing text such as utility bills, recipes, product labels, charts, and maps.

Word Attack
Learners predict words using pictures and meaning cues as well as attending to letter patterns and sounds.

© CP Images

People
Clara Hughes

Mini-Lesson: Making Inferences

Literacy Practice: TV Guide

© iStockphoto/Patricia Hofmeester

▶▶ Discussion

One moment can change a person's life. Do you agree? Why or why not?

Clara Hughes was born in Winnipeg, Manitoba. She is an Olympic athlete. Clara won medals in the Summer and Winter Olympic Games. She is the first Canadian to win medals in both Games.

Read the passage on the next two pages. Learn what moment changed Clara's life.

Clara Hughes

Clara was a teenager. She drank and smoked a lot. She took drugs. Clara did not care about anything.

Then Clara watched the 1988 Winter Olympics on TV. After that, Clara had a goal. She wanted to skate for Canada as a speed skater. She started to train.

Stop and Think:

Imagine you are Clara. What do you do to start training?

In 1990 a cycling coach talked to Clara. He wanted her to cycle. He thought Clara could be one of the best in the world. So Clara trained as a cyclist.

Clara cycled for Canada at the 1996 Summer Olympics. She won two bronze medals. Then Clara went back to her dream of speed skating for Canada. She won a gold medal in the 2006 Winter Olympics. She won bronze medals in 2002 and 2010.

At age 37, Clara knew it was time to move on. Now Clara has another goal. She wants to give all children a chance to dream.

Stop and Think:

What do you think Clara wants children to dream about?

Clara works with children who are at risk. She works with groups that help these children play sports. "Sports saved my life," says Clara. Clara thinks sports can help others, too. She is helping to make that happen.

© iStockphoto

. . . .

▶▶ Check the Facts

1. What were Clara's two goals? Did she reach those goals? Check the passage to find the answer.

2. What is the most important idea in the passage?

   (a) Clara is an Olympic athlete who helps children.

   (b) Clara won two medals in the 1996 Summer Games.

▶▶ Discussion

1. What do you think "children who are at risk" means?

2. Think about a special moment in your life. Describe the moment. How did that moment change your life?

3. Clara gives back to society. She works with children who are at risk. How do other people give back to society?

Mini-Lesson: Making Inferences

Look at the photo.
What is the man's job?

Did you guess a clown? How did you know?

1. You have a picture of a clown in your mind. Your picture comes from what you know about clowns.

2. The photo has clues that show the man is a clown. For example, the man has a painted clown face.

People often make guesses about what they see. These guesses are called inferences. People also make inferences when they read.

© BigStockPhoto/Steve Snowden

Read the paragraph in the box.
What is the person's job?

Did you say a trainer or a coach? Good for you. You made an inference. What did you already know about trainers or coaches? Which clues helped you make the inference?

I spend hours at the ice rink.
I work with young skaters.
I give them tips on how to skate faster.

Writers do not tell us everything.
So active readers make inferences as they read.

Read the sentences. Say or write an inference.
Explain why you made each inference.
The first one is an example.

What I saw	My inference	Why I made my inference
The lady wore boots and a heavy coat.	I think it was winter.	Because I know that it is cold in winter. Boots and coats keep people warm.
1. He wiped the sweat from his face.	I think	Because I know that
2. The leaves were falling from the trees.	I think	Because I know that

Now read the sentence about Clara. Say or write an inference.
Explain why you made the inference.
The first one is an example.

What I read	My inference	Why I made my inference
Clara took drugs as a teenager.	I think Clara hung out with bad friends.	Because I know that teens copy what their friends do.
Clara won a gold medal in the 2006 Olympics.	I think	Because I know that

Literacy Practice: TV Guide

A TV guide has a lot of information. To find a TV program, you do not need to read every word. You just need to know how to find information.

© BigStockPhoto/Johnnie Runner

The information in a TV guide is often in a table. To read a table, you need to look at these parts:

- title

- the headings at the top of the table

- the headings along the side of the table

These parts of a table help you find information quickly.

Look at the TV guide on page 7.
Find the title and headings.
Answer these questions:

1. (a) When can you watch all of these TV programs?

   (i) morning   (ii) afternoon   (iii) evening

   (b) What do the headings along the top of the TV guide tell you?

   (i) times   (ii) channels   (iii) program names

   (c) What do the headings along the side tell you?

   (i) times   (ii) channels   (iii) program names

2. (a) Which program starts at 9:00 on channel 2? Copy it here: _____

   (b) At what time does this program end? _____

3. (a) Which two channels show movies? _____ and _____

(b) *Singing Idol* comes on at 10:00 on two channels.

Which channels? _____ and _____

▶▶ Discussion

4. You want to watch *Three Silly Men* at 10:00. You do not get channel 7. What can you do?

5. It is 8:30. Which channel would you watch?

Headings

Title

March 3: Evening Programs

	8:30	9:00	9:30	10:00	10:30	11:00
2	Sad Sue	Crime Stop		Singing Idol		News
3	Olympics			Sports Report		Poker Club
4	Breaking News Report	Star Talk		Dance with the Stars		Star Talk
6	Giggles and Laughs	Crime Stop		Singing Idol		Chat Show
7	Olympics			Three Silly Men	Ugly Billy	World News Now
11	Movie (Thriller)			Movie (Comedy)		
22	Movie (Drama)			Movie (Thriller)		
24	Yoga Time	TV Yoga	Power Walk	Three Silly Men	Ugly Billy	Fit and Trim

7

Word Attack 1: Predict the Word

Look at each picture. Finish the sentence.
Think of a word that makes sense.
Say or write your word.

1. Clara helps _____.

2. _____ is a sport in the Summer Olympic Games.

Finish the sentences. Think of a word that makes sense.
Say or write your word.

1. Many people _____ the Olympics on TV.

2. Athletes train hard to win an Olympic _____.

3. The athletes come from many _____ around the world.

4. _____ helps athletes be their best in sports.

Word Attack 2: Word Families

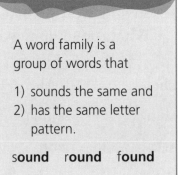

A word family is a group of words that

1) sounds the same and
2) has the same letter pattern.

sound **r**ound **f**ound

Look at the words in the box below.
Group the words into three word families.
Each word family has the same letter pattern.

The first one is an example.

train ✓	same	fast	name
game	rain	came	cast
last	past	pain	gain

ain   **ame**   **ast**

train _____ _____ _____

_____ _____ _____

_____ _____ _____

_____ _____ _____

Read each sentence.
Circle two words that have the bolded letter pattern.

ain   1. She works hard in the gym. "No pain, no gain," she says.

ame   2. Clara won medals at the Games. Now we all know her name.

ast   3. She skates fast. She skates past all the other skaters.

Word Attack 3: Digraphs

A. Say the words. Focus on the bolded digraphs.
What sound do the digraphs make?

> A digraph is two letters together that make one sound.

she	fre**sh**	**sh**op
think	no**th**ing	pa**th**
write	**wr**ap	**wr**ote

B. Finish the words in the sentences.
Think of a word that makes sense. Say or write your word.

1. I can't reach. I'm too *sh_____*.

2. These *sh_____* hurt my feet.

3. *Th_____* - you for your help.

4. Relax! Take a deep _____*th*.

5. That's not right. It's *wr_____*.

6. I fell and hurt my *wr_____*.

Are your words in this box? If yes, check your spelling.

wrist	Thank	short
breath	shoes	wrong

C. Read the sentences out loud.
Circle two words that have the bolded digraph.

sh 1. Sports shaped Clara's life. Clara says all children should be able to play sports.

th 2. Clara does many different things. She is a great athlete.

wr 3. Clara is a writer. She has written about her goals and dreams.

© BigStockPhoto/Jamie Wilson

© CP Images 2010

People
Alex Bilodeau

Mini-Lesson: Making Inferences

Literacy Practice: Work Schedule

© BigStockPhoto/Konstantin Shishkin

▶▶ Discussion

When one door closes in life, another door opens. What does this sentence mean to you?

Alex Bilodeau is an Olympic athlete. He is from Montreal, Quebec. In 2010, Alex won his first medal for Canada.

Read the passage on the next two pages. Learn what door closed and what door opened for Alex.

Alex Bilodeau

As a child, Alex loved to play hockey. Alex spent more time at the rink than with his family. His mom asked him to hang up his skates. Alex quit hockey. But he found a new love—skiing. Alex and his family skied together.

Stop and Think:

Imagine you are Alex. How do you feel about your mom's decision? Why?

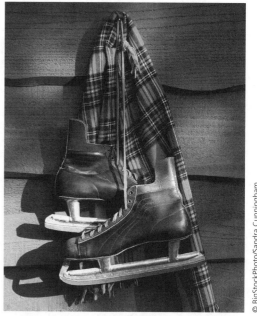

© BigStockPhoto/Sandra Cunningham

Alex began to compete in freestyle ski races. The ski hills were full of moguls. Alex skied around these bumps of snow. He skied with great speed. He learned to jump, flip, and twist in the air.

In 2006, Alex competed in the Winter Olympics. He was only 18 years old. Alex wanted to win a gold medal for Canada. He finished in 11th place. Alex trained harder.

© iStockphoto/Marco Rossetti

Alex competed in the 2010 Winter Olympics. These Games were held in Canada. More than 8,000 people came to watch Alex. Alex reached his goal, and won. More than that, Alex made sports history. He was the first Canadian to win Olympic gold on home soil. The crowd went wild! Alex's family went wild!

Stop and Think:

What do you think "home soil" means?

© Flickr/rymndhng

Alex's brother, Frederic, is proud of Alex. Frederic has cerebral palsy. Simple things like walking across a room are hard. Frederic does not complain. Alex says his brother inspires him to train hard. Both brothers say there is no limit to what a person can do.

Cerebral palsy is caused by damage to the brain, usually at birth. The person loses control of muscles and movement.

▶▶ Check the Facts

1. Alex competed in the 2006 and 2010 Olympic Games. Compare how he skied in those two Games. Check the passage to find the answer.

2. What is the the most important idea in the passage?

   (a) Alex had to quit hockey.

   (b) Alex worked hard to win an Olympic medal.

▶▶ Discussion

1. What do you think the word "inspire" means?

2. Describe a time when a door closed in your life. What new door opened? How did your life change?

3. Alex and Frederic say there is no limit to what a person can do. Do you agree with Alex and Frederic? Why or why not?

Mini-Lesson: Making Inferences

The writer does not always tell readers everything.
So readers make inferences.

You can make an inference by using what you already
know and by looking for clues in the text.

Read the sentences about Alex.
Say or write an inference.
Explain why you made each inference.

The first one is an example.

What I read	My inference	Why I made my inference
Alex and his family skied together.	I think Alex's family had money.	Because I know that skiing costs a lot of money.
1. Alex finished 11th. He trained harder.	I think	Because I know that
2. Alex learned to jump, flip, and twist in the air on skis.	I think	Because I know that

Frederic and Alex

Frederic is proud of his brother, Alex.
And Alex is just as proud of Frederic.

Read the paragraphs about Frederic.
Say or write an inference about Frederic.
Explain why you made each inference.

Alex hugs Frederic.

Paragraph 1

Alex skied on a hill with moguls.
Frederic wanted to ski on the same
hill. Frederic fell about 50 times. But
he kept getting up.

My inference:

I think Frederic _____

_____ .

Paragraph 2

A reporter asked Frederic, "What one
thing would you like to do that you
can't do?" Frederic said he would like
to be a fireman.

My inference:

I think Frederic _____

_____ .

Literacy Practice: Work Schedule

People use schedules every day. Schedules help people organize their time.

To read a schedule, you need to look at the title and the headings. Some schedules use short forms. For example, the word *Sunday* becomes *Sun*. Some schedules have a key. The key tells you what the short forms stand for.

6:09 PM	6:15
6:49 PM	6:
7:26 PM	7
7:56 PM	7
8:26 PM	8:
8:56 PM	8:5

Look at the schedule below.
Find the title, headings, and key.
Then answer the questions on page 17.

Title

Headings

**Shift Schedule
(May 8 to May 14)**

	Sun May 8	Mon May 9	Tues May 10	Wed May 11	Thurs May 12	Fri May 13	Sat May 14
7:30 am – 3:00 pm	Bud **T** Don **FP** May **D**	Shar **T** Sam **FP** Pat **D**	Shar **T** Sam **FP** Pat **D**	Shar **T** Sam **FP** Pat **D**	Pat **T** Sam **FP** Shar **D**	Pat **T** Sam **FP** Shar **D**	Bud **T** Don **FP** May **D**
Noon – 3:00 pm	(Closed)	Lisa **T**	Lisa **T**	Lisa **T**	Lisa **T**	Stef **T**	Stef **T**
2:30 pm – 7:30 pm	(Closed)	Stef **T** Mika **D**	Stef **T** Mika **D**	Stef **T** Mika **D**	Biff **T** Mika **D**	Biff **T** Mika **FP** Lisa **D**	Biff **T** Mika **FP** Lisa **D**

T = Tables
FP = Food Prep
D = Dishes

Key

1. (a) What is the schedule for?   (i) coffee breaks   (ii) shifts   (iii) holidays

    (b) How much time does the schedule cover?

        (i) one day   (ii) one week   (iii) one month

2. (a) What do the headings across the top of the schedule tell you?

                                (i) days and dates   (ii) jobs to do   (iii) shift times

    (b) What do the headings along the side tell you?

                                (i) days and dates   (ii) jobs to do   (iii) shift times

3. Which shift is the shortest? Copy the time here: _____

4. Look at the key. What short form is used for *tables*? Copy it here: _____

5. Imagine you are Lisa.

    (a) Do you have to work on Sunday?   Yes   No

    (b) How many days are you working this week? _____

    (c) What shift are you working on Friday? Copy the time here: _____

    (d) What is your job on Saturday?   (i) tables   (ii) food prep   (iii) dishes

    (e) How many hours are you working this week? _____

▶▶ Discussion

6. Think about your life. Which shift would work best for you?

Word Attack 1: Predict the Word

**Look at each picture. Finish the sentence.
Think of a word that makes sense.
Say or write your word.**

1. This move looks _____.

2. The crowd _____.

**Finish the sentences. Think of a word that makes sense.
Say or write your word.**

1. Many _____ like playing sports.

2. Hockey and _____ are winter sports.

3. Cycling and _____ are summer sports.

4. Playing sports makes a person _____.

PEOPLE

Word Attack 2: Word Families

Look at the words in the box below.
Group the words into three word families.
Each word family has the same letter pattern.

The first one is an example.

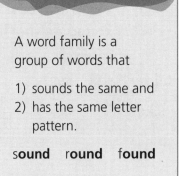

A word family is a group of words that

1) sounds the same and
2) has the same letter pattern.

sound   round   found

hang ✓	hate	sang	dump
skate	late	date	bang
bump	jump	rang	lump

ang   **ate**   **ump**

hang _____   _____   _____

_____   _____   _____

_____   _____   _____

_____   _____   _____

Read each sentence.
Circle two words that have the bolded letter pattern.

ang   1. A buzzer rang. A gun went bang. The race started.

ate   2. Fans hate when a game starts late.

ump   3. Sometimes skiers cannot jump. Machines have to
         dump fake snow on the hill.

Word Attack 3: Digraphs

A. Say the words. Focus on the bolded digraphs.
What sound do the digraphs make?

> A digraph is two letters together that make one sound.

child   rea**ch**es   ri**ch**

ho**ck**ey   si**ck**   pu**ck**

why   **wh**at   **wh**en

B. Finish the words in the sentences.
Think of a word that makes sense. Say or write your word.

1. Do you have any spare *ch_____*?

2. I love fish and *ch_____*.

3. Help! The door is _____*ck*.

4. His hockey _____*ck* broke in half.

5. *Wh_____* do you live?

6. *Wh_____* ones do you want?

Are your words in this box?
If yes, check your spelling.

chips	Which	Where
stuck	change	stick

C. Read the sentences out loud.
Circle two words that have the bolded digraph.

ch   1. Alex does not choose to ski. But skiing changes his life.

ck   2. Alex is lucky. His family backs him all the way.

wh   3. Alex's family cheers while he whips down the ski hill.

© CP images 2010

Relationships
The List

Mini-Lesson: Main Idea and Details

Literacy Practice: Pamphlet

▶▶ Discussion

Think about the last time you talked to a doctor. How did you feel after talking to the doctor?

> Better?
> Confused?
> Upset?

Why did you feel this way?

Read the passage on the next two pages. Learn why Anna feels upset after she sees the doctor.

The List

Anna is not feeling well. She visits a doctor. When Anna leaves the office, she feels upset. She is mad at herself. That night Anna calls a friend. "I saw the doctor today," Anna says. "I forgot to tell him about my headaches. I forgot to tell him I'm not sleeping well."

Stop and Think:

How do you think Anna felt as she talked to the doctor? Explain your answer.

"I will help you," says Anna's friend. "We will make a list. Then you will not forget what you want to say to the doctor."

The next time Anna sees the doctor, she is ready. "How are you?" the doctor asks.

"Not that great," Anna says. "I have a list of things I want to talk about."

"Oh," the doctor says. He looked surprised.

Anna takes out the list she made with her friend. "I do not want to forget anything," she says. The doctor looks at his watch.

"Well, what is on your list?" he asks.

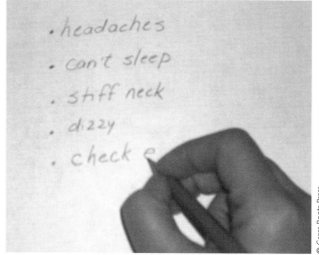

Stop and Think:

What do you think the doctor is thinking and feeling? Explain your answer.

Anna tells the doctor about her headaches. She talks about everything on her list. The doctor takes notes. Sometimes he stops Anna to ask a question. When Anna gets to the end of her list, the doctor says, "I think you should have some tests."

Anna smiles. The list did the trick. The doctor is going to help her.

· · · · · · · · · · · · · · · ·

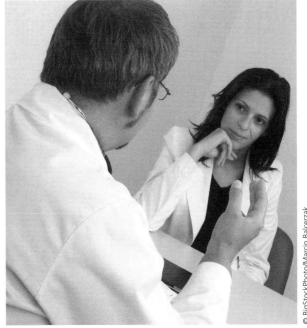

© BigStockPhoto/Marcin Balcerzak

▶▶ Check the Facts

1. Compare Anna's first visit to the doctor with her second visit to the doctor. Check the passage to find the answer.

2. What is the most important idea in the passage?

(a) Doctors will help you only if you have a list.

(b) Visits to the doctor are better when you are prepared.

▶▶ Discussion

1. How do you know that Anna and her friend are close friends?

2. Would you take a list to the doctor's office? Why or why not?

3. The list made it easier for Anna to talk with her doctor. What else can people do to make visits to a doctor better? How can doctors make visits better?

Mini-Lesson: Main Idea and Details

Active readers look for main ideas and details.

Main ideas are important ideas.

Details support the main ideas. Details help readers

(1) understand the main ideas and

(2) remember the main ideas.

Read the main ideas in the chart.
Check two details for each main idea.
The first one is an example.

Main idea	Details
It rains a lot every spring.	(a)___ It is warm outside. (b)_✔_ The rivers flood. (c)_✔_ The dirt roads wash away.
1. My friend helps me a lot.	(a)___ She picks up my son from school. (b)___ She lives close to me. (c)___ She feeds my cat when I'm away.
2. People use parks in many ways.	(a)___ Some people have picnics. (b)___ Some people take long walks. (c)___ Some people do not like parks.
3. The Olympic Games are popular.	(a)___ Millions of people watch the Games. (b)___ The Games cost a lot of money. (c)___ Thousands of people go to the Games.

Read the main ideas in the chart.
The main ideas are about Anna.
Check two details for each main idea.

Main idea	Details
1. Anna is not happy when she leaves the doctor's office.	(a)___ She feels upset. (b)___ She is mad at herself. (c)___ She visits the doctor.
2. Anna forgets to tell the doctor some things.	(a)___ She is not sleeping well. (b)___ She leaves the office. (c)___ She has headaches.
3. Anna has a good friend.	(a)___ She tells her friend about her health. (b)___ Her friend is not a doctor. (c)___ Her friend helps Anna write a list.
4. Anna is ready for her next visit to the doctor.	(a)___ She sees the same doctor. (b)___ She has her list. (c)___ She does not forget anything.
5. The doctor listens to Anna.	(a)___ He takes notes. (b)___ He asks questions. (c)___ He looks at his watch.

Literacy Practice:
Pamphlet

Health clinics often have free pamphlets. Pamphlets talk about many health topics. For example, pamphlets talk about flus and colds.

Most pamphlets have these parts: a title

headings

pictures

These parts give you clues about what is in the pamphlet.

Look at the pamphlet on page 27.
Read the title. Read the headings. Look at the pictures.
Then mark the following statements true (T) or false (F).

1. The pamphlet is about the flu. _____

2. The pamphlet has four headings. _____

3. The pamphlet tells you how to treat a cold. _____

4. There are only three ways to protect yourself from colds. _____

5. You should sneeze into your sleeve. _____

6. Stay home if you want to stop your cold from spreading. _____

▶▶ Discussion

7. You wake up one morning with a sore throat. Should you see a doctor?

Title

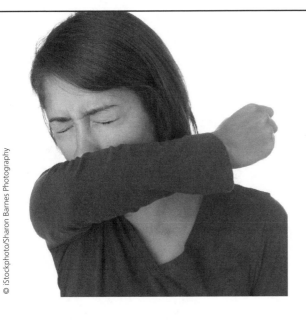

© iStockphoto/Sharon Barnes Photography

The Common Cold

Headings

What causes a cold?

A cold comes from a virus. A cold virus can spread when people cough, sneeze, or shake hands.

How can I protect myself from colds?

- Wash your hands often.
- Keep your hands away from your face.
- Eat well.
- Get plenty of rest.
- Exercise.

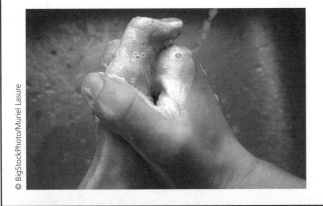

© BigStockPhoto/Muriel Lasure

How can I stop my cold from spreading?

- Wash your hands often.
- Cough and sneeze into your sleeve.
- Stay home.

What can I do to feel better?

- Stay home and rest.
- Drink plenty of water and juice.
- Drink hot tea with lemon and honey.
- Gargle with warm salt water.
- Don't smoke or drink alcohol.

Should I see a doctor?

- Do you have an earache?
- Do you feel pain in your forehead?
- Is your fever above 39°C?
- Is your throat still sore after 7 days?
- Do you feel short of breath?

If you said "yes" to any of these questions, see a doctor.

For more information, call (800) 555-5555

Word Attack 1: Predict the Word

Look at each picture. Finish the sentence.
Think of a word that makes sense.
Say or write your word.

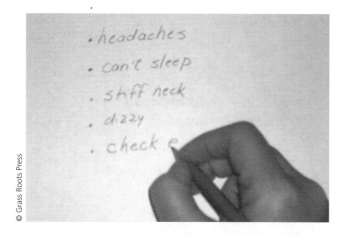

1. Anna _____ a list.

2. This woman has a bad _____.

Finish the sentences. Think of a word that makes sense.
Say or write your word.

1. We need to tell the doctor about our _____ problems.

2. I ate something bad. Now my _____ hurts.

3. I think I'm _____ to dust. I sneeze all the time.

4. I fell on my arm. Now I have a big black and blue _____.

RELATIONSHIPS

Word Attack 2: Word Families

Look at the words in the box below.
Group the words into three word families.
Each word family has the same letter pattern.

The first one is an example.

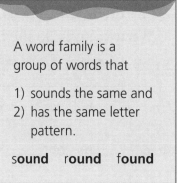

A word family is a
group of words that

1) sounds the same and
2) has the same letter
   pattern.

sound   **round**   **found**

think ✓	rest	wink	nest
take	make	best	lake
test	sink	pink	shake

ink   **ake**   **est**

think

Read the sentences.
Circle two words that have the bolded letter pattern.

ink   1.   I think these pink pills are too strong. I feel dizzy.

ake   2.   Should I shake the bottle before I take the medicine?

est   3.   Is this the best test for checking my heart?

Word Attack 3: Blends

> Blends are two or three consonants put together. You can hear the sound that goes with each consonant.

A. Say the words. Focus on the bolded blends.
   What sounds do the bolded blends make?
   Say or write a new word that has the same blend.

sleep   **sl**ed   **sl**ide   _____

smile   **sm**other   **sm**oke   _____

trick   **tr**ain   **tr**avel   _____

B. Finish the words in the sentences.
   Think of a word that makes sense. Say or write your word.

1. Please don't *sl*_____ the door.

2. Not so fast! *Sl*_____ down!

3. You think you're so *sm*_____ .

4. What's that stinky *sm*_____?

5. I can't *tr*_____ you. You lie.

6. They cut down all the *tr*_____ .

Are your words in this box? If yes, check your spelling.

slam	smart	trust
smell	trees	slow

C. Read the sentences out loud.
   Circle two words that have the bolded blend.

sl   1. Don't eat your fruit. Slurp it! Slice it up.
          Add some milk. And blend.

sm   2. Drink a small fruit smoothie every day.

tr   3. The trick is to try to use fresh fruit. Yum!

RELATIONSHIPS

UNIT 4

Relationships
The Phone Call

Mini-Lesson: Main Idea and Details

Literacy Practice: Cheque

▶▶ Discussion

Many people rent houses or apartments. Describe three common problems that tenants have.

What steps can tenants take to fix these problems?

Read the passage on the next two pages. Learn why Jenny is not happy with her landlord.

The Phone Call

Jenny is happy with her apartment. Jenny likes her apartment because she can walk to many places. She can walk to work and to stores. She can walk to the daycare with her son.

But Jenny is not happy with her landlord. She wants him to fix the stove. She calls him, but he does not call her back.

Stop and Think:

What do you think Jenny does next? Read on. Are your ideas in the passage?

Jenny asks her neighbour for help. The neighbour tells Jenny about a place that helps tenants. Jenny goes to the office and talks to a woman. The woman tells Jenny about tenants' rights. The woman tells Jenny what to do.

The next day, Jenny calls her landlord again. He does not answer, so Jenny leaves a message. She says, "Hi, Glen. It's Jenny again. I know you are busy. But I need you to fix my stove. I spoke to a woman about tenant's rights. I'm going to mail you a copy of a letter I wrote. The letter tells you what is wrong with my stove. If you don't fix it, I can take legal steps. Please call me back. Thanks."

Stop and Think:

Imagine you are Jenny's landlord. How do you feel about this message? Why?

Two hours later the phone rings. It is Jenny's landlord. He says, "I'll fix the stove tomorrow."

· · · · · · · · · · · · · · · · · ·

▶▶ Check the Facts

1. What does Jenny learn about dealing with landlords? Check the passage to find the answer.

2. What is the most important idea in the passage?

(a) Write letters to your landlord.

(b) Know your rights as a tenant.

▶▶ Discussion

1. Why do you think the landlord does not call Jenny back after her first message?

2. What was the last thing you had to fix in your home? How did it get fixed? What went right? What went wrong? What did you learn?

3. Landlords and tenants need to treat each other fairly. What can landlords do to be fair to tenants? What can tenants do to be fair to landlords?

Mini-Lesson: Main Idea and Details

Main ideas are important ideas.

Details support the main ideas.

Details help readers   (1) understand the main ideas and

(2) remember the main ideas.

Read the main ideas in the chart.
The main ideas are about Jenny.
Check two details for each main idea.

Main idea	Details
1. Jenny likes her apartment.	(a)___ She can walk to work and to stores. (b)___ She has a stove. (c)___ She can walk to the daycare with her son.
2. Jenny asks for help.	(a)___ She talks on the phone. (b)___ She talks to a woman in an office. (c)___ She talks to her neighbour.
3. Jenny learns how to deal with her landlord.	(a)___ She must be firm. (b)___ She learns about her rights as a tenant. (c)___ She can leave a message for the landlord.
4. Jenny gives the landlord a chance to fix the stove.	(a)___ She mails the landlord a letter. (b)___ She is not happy with the landlord. (c)___ She leaves the landlord two messages.

Read the paragraphs. The main ideas are bolded.
As you read, underline two details for each main idea.

Paragraph 1

Sal's apartment has some problems. It
is too small. Sal has nowhere to put his
things. The tenants next door are noisy.
They play their music late at night. They
have loud fights all the time. Sal can't sleep.

Paragraph 2

It was Sal's birthday. He went outside. His
car was gone. Sal phoned the police. The
police told Sal his car was stolen. Sal took
a bus to the police station. Sal got off the
bus. He slipped and broke his leg. **Sal had a
bad birthday.**

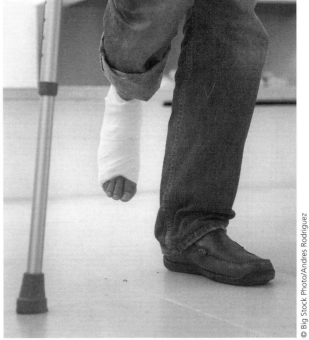

Literacy Practice: Cheque

People can use cheques to pay their rent.
Paying by cheque is safer than paying in
cash. Paying by cheque also gives people
proof of payment.

A cheque contains a lot of information.
A cheque tells you

- how much the cheque is for
- who can cash the cheque
- what the cheque is for
- who the cheque is from

Cheque

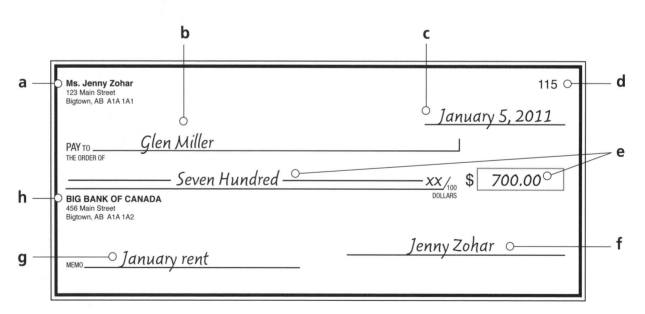

Look at the cheque on page 36.
Where can you find information to answer the questions below?
Put the correct letter in each blank.

The first one is an example.

1. Who can cash the cheque? __b__

2. How much is the cheque for? _____

3. What is the cheque for? _____

4. Who sent the cheque? _____

5. When can the cheque be cashed? _____

6. Who signed the cheque? _____

7. What is the number of the cheque? _____

8. Which bank does the cheque come from? _____

▶▶ Discussion

9. Do you use cheques? Why or why not?

10. Should a person use a pen or a pencil to fill out a cheque? Give a reason for your answer.

11. A blank cheque does not show how much money the cheque is for. Should a person sign a blank cheque? Why or why not?

Word Attack 1: Predict the Word

Look at each picture. Finish the sentence.
Think of a word that makes sense.
Say or write your word.

1. Jenny lives in a small
   _____.

2. The woman showed Jenny
   the _____.

Finish the sentences. Think of a word that makes sense.
Say or write your word.

1. Leave a _____ if nobody answers the phone.

2. I told my _____ that the heat would not come on.

3. My one-year-old son is at a _____ while I work.

4. I want to paint the walls because I don't like the _____.

RELATIONSHIPS

Word Attack 2: Word Families

Look at the words in the box below.
Look for letter patterns.
Group the words into three word families.

The first one is an example.

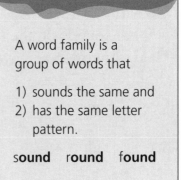

A word family is a group of words that

1) sounds the same and
2) has the same letter pattern.

sound   round   found

back ✓	race	stack	fell
place	sell	face	crack
tell	pack	well	trace

ack   **ace**   **ell**

back   _____   _____

_____   _____   _____

_____   _____   _____

_____   _____   _____

Read the sentences.
Circle two words that have the bolded letter pattern.

ack   1. The back bedroom has a big crack in the wall.

ace   2. There is no trace of damage in my place.

ell   3. Tell the landlord that the washer does not work well.

Word Attack 3: Blends

> Blends are two or three consonants put together. You can hear the sound that goes with each consonant.

A. Say the words. Focus on the bolded blends.
What sounds do the bolded blends make?
Say or write a new word that has the same blend.

place	**pl**ease	ex**pl**ain	_____
Glen	**gl**ow	**gl**obe	_____
from	**fr**ee	**fr**iend	_____

B. Finish the words in the sentences.
Think of a word that makes sense. Say or write your word.

1. Think ahead. Make a *pl*_____.

2. Two *pl*_____two is four.

3. Don't be sad. Be *gl*_____.

4. It's cold. Put on your *gl*_____.

5. Let's go out next *Fr*_____.

6. Eat *fr*_____ fruit every day.

Are your words in this box? If yes, check your spelling.

Friday	plan	gloves
glad	plus	fresh

C. Read the sentences out loud.
Circle two words that have the bolded blend.

pl 1. A plumber will fix a plugged sink.

gl 2. Hot, soapy water will take glue off glass.

fr 3. A landlord should stop pipes from freezing in the winter.

© iStockphoto.com/LisaFX Photographic Designs

Health and Safety
The Burn

© Grass Roots Press

Mini-Lesson: Sequencing

Literacy Practice: Chart

© BigStockPhoto/Graca Victoria

▶▶ Discussion

Some burns are serious. A doctor must treat them. Other burns are minor. You can treat them at home.

How do people get minor burns?

Read the passage on the next two pages. Learn who treats John's minor burn.

The Burn

"Ow!" John yells. The steam from the boiling water rises from the pot. John's fingers feel like they are on fire. He rushes to the kitchen sink and turns on the cold water.

John sticks his hand under the running water. He looks at his red fingers. John hopes his skin will cool quickly because the burn is very painful. He keeps his hand under the water for 15 minutes.

Stop and Think:

For how long would you keep your hand under running water?

John uses a clean dish towel to dry his wet hand. But he lets the air dry his burned fingers. "Mina," John calls, "I need your help! I burned my fingers!"

"Oh no, Dad! Not again!" Mina says, getting off the couch.

Mina washes her hands before grabbing the first aid kit. She takes out a roll of clean cloth and first aid tape. She gently tapes the cloth over John's burned fingers.

Stop and Think:

Why do you think Mina washes her hands?

HEALTH AND SAFETY

"I do not see any blisters," Mina says. "The burn does not look serious."

"Thanks, little one," says John. "You are my ten-year-old doctor."

"You should be more careful, Dad," says Mina. "I like your cooking, but you are burning yourself too often. The next time I make a house call, I am going to send you a bill!"

. . . .

▶▶ Check the Facts

1. What steps do John and Mina take to treat John's burn? Check the passage to find the answer.

2. What is the most important idea in the passage?

   (a) It is not hard to treat a minor burn.

   (b) Be careful when you are cooking.

▶▶ Discussion

1. What words would you use to describe (a) John and (b) Mina? Give a reason for your answers.

2. Describe a time you treated a minor burn. How did the person get the burn? How did you treat the burn?

3. Do you have a first aid kit at home? What do you keep in it? What do you need to add to it? How can you find out what to keep in a first aid kit?

Mini-Lesson: Sequencing

Good writers use a plan to develop their ideas. One kind of plan is sequencing. Writers use sequencing to

(1) tell us how to do things and

(2) put things in the order they happen.

> Writers help readers follow a sequence. Writers use word clues such as **first**, **then**, **while**, and **finally**.

The steps below tell you how to make a cup of tea.
Put the steps in sequence.

_____ While the water heats up, put a teabag in a cup.

_____ Then pour the boiled water into the cup.

_____ First, put water on to boil.

_____ Finally, add milk and sugar.

Circle the words that helped you put the steps in sequence.

The steps below tell you how to treat a burn.
Put the steps in sequence.
The first step is done for you.

_____ Finally, tape clean cloth over the burn.

__1__ Hold the burn under cool running water.

_____ When the burn is dry, cover it with clean cloth.

_____ Then let the air dry the burned area.

Circle the words that helped you put the steps in sequence.

Active readers look for the writer's plan. Knowing the writer's plan helps readers understand the writer's ideas.

The Aloe Vera Plant

Some people have aloe vera plants. They use the aloe vera plant for skin care. For example, they use the plant to ease the pain of sunburns.

Read the paragraph below.
Then answer the questions.

It is easy to use the aloe vera plant. First, cut a small piece off the plant. Next, slice the piece down the middle. Then squeeze it. The juice inside the piece of aloe will ooze out. Rub the juice on your skin. Your sunburn will feel less painful.

1. What is the paragraph telling you how to do?
   Circle the right answer.

   (a) how to cut aloe vera plants

   (b) how to get a sunburn

   (c) how to use the aloe vera plant

2. Read the paragraph again.
   Circle the words that helped you follow the sequence.

Literacy Practice: Chart

People use charts to put ideas in order. Charts often compare two or more things. For example, a chart can compare two cities. Or a chart can compare three types of food—fast food, homemade food, and restaurant food.

To read a chart, you need to look at these parts:

- the title

- the headings at the top of the chart

- the headings at the side of the chart

The title tells you what is being compared.

The headings organize the information.

Look at the chart on page 47.
Read the title. Read the headings.
Then answer these questions:

1. What is the title of the chart? Copy it here: _____

2. The chart compares three types of burns. One type is a first-degree burn. What are the other two types of burn? Write the names here:

   (a) _____ (b) _____

3. The chart compares burns in two ways. What are the two ways?

   (a) _____

   (b) _____

4. Mark the following statements true (T) or false (F).

(a) First-degree burns swell and sting. _____

(b) You should break blisters. _____

(c) It is a good idea to use ice or butter on burns. _____

(d) Call for help if you have a third-degree burn. _____

▶▶ Discussion

5. How are first-degree burns and second-degree burns different from each other?

Title

Headings

Types of Burns

Type of burn	How the burn looks and feels	How to treat the burn
First-degree	Burned skin is red Some swelling Some pain or stinging	Hold burned skin under cool water until pain goes away. Cover the burn lightly with clean cloth.
Second-degree	Burned skin is very red Lots of swelling Lots of pain Blisters form	Do not use ice. Do not use butter or creams. Do not break blisters.
Third-degree	Burned area is black, or white and dry	Call 911. Raise burned body part. Cover burn with cool, damp cloth or towel. Do not remove burned clothes from burned body part. Do not put burned body part in cold water.

Source: www.mayoclinic.com, January 5, 2010.

Word Attack 1: Predict the Word

Look at each picture. Finish the sentence.
Think of a word that makes sense.
Say or write your word.

1. John uses a _____ to dry his hand.

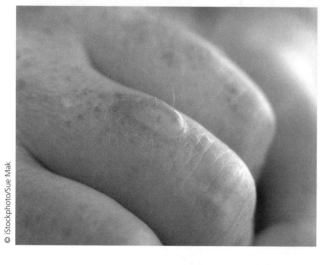

2. A second-degree burn may cause a _____.

Finish the sentences. Think of a word that makes sense.
Say or write your word.

1. She grabbed the hot pot and burned all of her _____ .

2. Be _____ when you are near a hot stove.

3. A minor burn turns red and _____ .

4. In an _____ , call 911.

HEALTH AND SAFETY

Word Attack 2: Word Families

Look at the words in the box below.
Look for letter patterns.
Group the words into three word families.

The first one is an example.

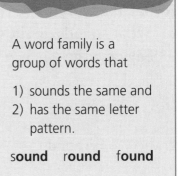

A word family is a group of words that

1) sounds the same and
2) has the same letter pattern.

sound   round   found

stick ✓	sing	pick	thing
bring	kick	cape	prick
tape	ring	drape	shape

ick   **ing**   **ape**

stick _____   _____   _____

_____   _____   _____

_____   _____   _____

_____   _____   _____

Read each sentence.
Circle two words that have the bolded letter pattern.

ick   1. Do not prick a blister. Do not stick a bandage on a burn.

ing   2. Bring the first aid kit here. How do we use this thing?

ape   3. He cut the cloth into the right shape. Then he used tape to hold it down.

Word Attack 3: Blends

> Blends are two or three consonants put together. You can hear the sound that goes with each consonant.

A. Say the words. Focus on the bolded blends.
What sounds do the bolded blends make?
Say or write a new word that has the same blend.

stove   **st**ick   **st**op   _____

grab   **gr**ound   **gr**een   _____

blister   **bl**ue   **bl**end   _____

B. Finish the words in the sentences.
Think of a word that makes sense. Say or write your word.

1. *St*_____ up for your rights!

2. The night sky is full of *st*_____.

3. I *gr*_____ flowers in pots.

4. Cut the *gr*_____.

5. I'm cold. Get me a *bl*_____.

6. He can't see. He is *bl*_____.

Are your words in this box?
If yes, check your spelling.

grass	stand	blind
blanket	grow	stars

C. Read the sentences out loud.
Circle two words that have the bolded blend.

st   1. A first-degree burn can sting a lot.

gr   2. A second-degree burn can cause great pain.

bl   3. A third-degree burn does not bleed. It turns black or white.

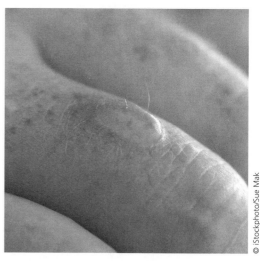

© iStockphoto/Sue Mak

HEALTH AND SAFETY

Health and Safety
Medicine

Mini-Lesson: Sequencing

Literacy Practice: Prescription Label

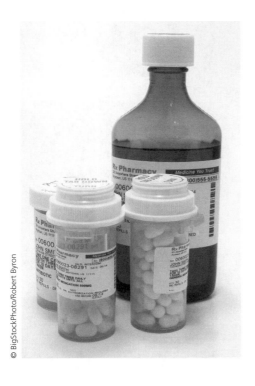

▶▶ Discussion

What should you know about medicine before you take it?

What if you have a question about your medicine? How do you find the answer?

Read the passage on the next two pages. Learn who answers Carla's questions about medicine.

Medicine

Carla is at the drugstore. She holds Tony because he is sick and crying. Five-year-old Becky is bored. They have waited in line for 15 minutes. At last, Carla gets to the counter. The pharmacist fills Carla's prescription. Now Carla can go home.

Carla reads the label on the medicine bottle. She must give Tony the medicine every eight hours. He sleeps a lot. Will Carla have to wake Tony up to give him the medicine? She is not sure. So Carla phones the drugstore.

Stop and Think:

Do you think Carla will have to wake Tony up?

"I have a question about my son's medicine," says Carla. The pharmacist at the drugstore is helpful. At the end of the phone call, Carla knows what to do.

Stop and Think:

Why do you think Carla phones the drugstore instead of her doctor?

For seven days, Carla gives Tony medicine every eight hours. Sometimes she has to wake him up. Every day, Carla watches Tony. She wants to make sure the medicine is working. Tony seems better. But Carla must give him the medicine until it is all gone.

HEALTH AND SAFETY

Finally, Tony is back to his playful self. Carla does not worry about him. The whole family will sleep better now.

• • • • • • • • • • • • • • • • •

▶▶ Check the Facts

1. What steps does Carla take when Tony gets sick? Check the passage to find the answer.

2. What is the most important idea in the passage?

(a) If you have to wait in line at a drugstore, be patient.

(b) If you have questions about medicine, ask a pharmacist.

▶▶ Discussion

1. Tony seems better. Why do you think Carla must keep giving Tony the medicine?

2. Think about the last time you needed to use medicine. How did you feel about using the medicine? Okay? Worried? Upset? Why did you feel this way?

3. Sometimes medicine causes side effects like headaches. What other side effects might medicine cause? Should people see a doctor if they suffer side effects from medicine? Why or why not?

Mini-Lesson: Sequencing

Good writers use a plan to develop their ideas. One kind of plan is sequencing. Writers use sequencing to

(1) tell us how to do things and

(2) put things in the order they happen.

> Writers help readers follow a sequence. Writers use word clues such as **first**, **then**, **while**, and **finally**.

The sentences below tell you Carla's story.
Put the sentences in sequence.

_____ After Carla got home, she phoned the drugstore.

_____ Finally, Tony was better.

_____ Then she gave Tony the medicine.

_____ First, Carla went to the drugstore to get medicine.

_____ After seven days, the medicine was all gone.

Circle the words that helped you put the sentences in sequence.

Carla's daughter, Becky, had a fever.
The sentences below tell you what Carla did.
Put the sentences in sequence.

_____ The next day, Becky's fever was gone.

_____ Then Carla phoned the doctor.

_____ First, Carla took Becky's temperature.

_____ While on the phone, Carla asked the doctor lots of questions.

Circle the words that helped you put the sentences in sequence.

The Smoker

Alex started to smoke at the age of 12.
At the age of 50, Alex said, "Enough! It's time to quit!"

Alex takes many steps to quit smoking.
Read the paragraph below.
Circle the words that help you follow the sequence.

Alex wanted to quit smoking. First, he threw his smokes away. Then he added up how much smokes cost him each month. It was a lot! After talking to his friends, Alex bought some nicotine gum. But the gum made Alex dizzy. Finally, Alex went to a clinic. The clinic helped Alex. Alex became a non-smoker.

Now put these steps in sequence.

_____ Alex bought nicotine gum.

_____ Alex threw his smokes away.

_____ Alex talked to his friends.

_____ Alex went to a clinic.

_____ Alex added up the cost of smoking.

Literacy Practice: Prescription Label

A prescription label tells you what you need to know about medicine. The label has information about

- who the prescription is for
- what the medicine is
- how to take the medicine
- how often to take the medicine

All prescription medicine must have labels. This is the law.

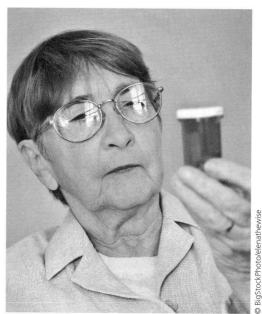

© BigStockPhoto/elenathewise

Prescription Label

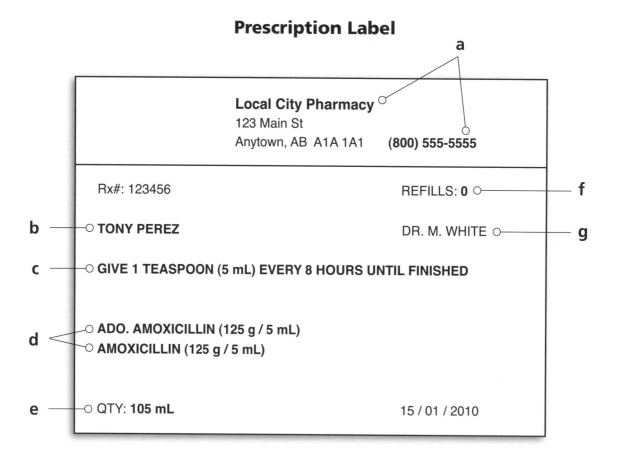

a

Local City Pharmacy
123 Main St
Anytown, AB A1A 1A1   **(800) 555-5555**

Rx#: 123456   REFILLS: **0** ──── **f**

b ──○ **TONY PEREZ**   DR. M. WHITE ○──── **g**

c ──○ **GIVE 1 TEASPOON (5 mL) EVERY 8 HOURS UNTIL FINISHED**

d ──○ **ADO. AMOXICILLIN (125 g / 5 mL)**
     ──○ **AMOXICILLIN (125 g / 5 mL)**

e ──○ QTY: **105 mL**   15 / 01 / 2010

Look at the prescription label on page 56.
Where can you find information to answer the questions below?
Put the correct letter in each blank.

The first one is an example.

1. Who is the prescription for? __b__

2. How much medicine should Carla give Tony? _____

3. How often should Carla give Tony the medicine? _____

4. Who is the doctor that wrote the prescription? _____

5. How many refills of medicine can Carla get? _____

6. What is the name of the drug in the medicine? _____

7. How can Carla contact the drugstore? _____

8. How much medicine is in the bottle? _____

▶▶ **Discussion**

9. Carla gave Tony a teaspoon of medicine at 10:00 a.m.
   When must she give Tony the next teaspoon of medicine?

   (a) 5:00 p.m.   (b) 6:00 p.m.   (c) 8:00 p.m.

   How did you figure out the answer?

10. A drugstore can be a busy place. So always check to make
    sure you get the right medicine. What information on the
    prescription label should you check?

Word Attack 1: Predict the Word

Look at each picture. Finish the sentence.
Think of a word that makes sense.
Say or write your word.

> What do you do if you can't read a word?
>
> Active readers think of a word that makes sense.

1. The _____ helps Carla.

2. Carla uses a _____ to give Tony the medicine.

Finish the sentences. Think of a word that makes sense.
Say or write your word.

1. We buy medicine at a _____ .

2. The _____ on the bottle tells us how to use the medicine.

3. Carla wipes Tony's nose with a _____ .

4. Tony has a fever. His _____ is over 37°C.

Word Attack 2: Word Families

Look at the words in the box below.
Group the words into three word families.
Each word family has the same letter pattern.

The first one is an example.

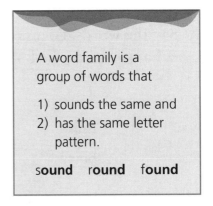

A word family is a
group of words that

1) sounds the same and
2) has the same letter
pattern.

sound   **round**   **found**

must ✓	light	fold	crust
night	told	just	right
hold	dust	might	sold

ust   **ight**   **old**

must _____   _____   _____

_____   _____   _____

_____   _____   _____

_____   _____   _____

Read each sentence.
Circle two words that have the bolded letter pattern.

ust   1. I must take just one pill every six hours.

ight   2. I keep a light on at night when my son is sick.

old   3. The doctor told me to hold my breath.

Word Attack 3: Long Vowel Sounds

A. Say the words. Focus on the bolded letters.
What sound do the bolded letters make?

make	name	case
wait	rain	snail
day	playful	pray

All the bolded letters make the long /a/ sound.

B. Finish the sentences. Use a word that has a long /a/ sound.
Think of a word that makes sense. Say or write your word.

1. It is not _____ to walk alone.

2. Don't cheat. It's just a _____.

3. The sink's _____ is plugged.

4. The killer is in _____ for life.

5. What a nice thing to _____!

6. My son uses _____ to colour.

Are your words in the box?
If yes, check your spelling.

say	game	safe
jail	crayons	drain

C. Read each sentence out loud.
Circle two words that have the long /a/ sound.

/a/   1. The label tells us to take two pills.

/ai/   2. Wait for the pain to stop.

/ay/ 3. It will go away within one day.

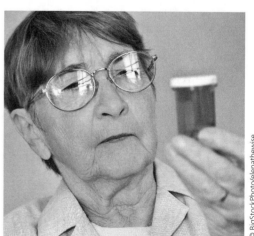

© BigStockPhoto/elenathewise

Environment

Avalanche!

Mini-Lesson: Cause and Effect

Literacy Practice: Thermometer

▶▶ **Discussion**

What do you know about avalanches?

Rogers Pass is in British Columbia. In 1910, an avalanche came down a mountain in Rogers Pass. The avalanche killed 58 men.

Read the passage on the next two pages. Learn why so many men died in the Rogers Pass avalanche.

Avalanche!

Avalanches have the power to destroy and kill. Avalanches can sweep trees down mountains. Avalanches can bury towns. They can trap people in snow.

On March 4, 1910, an avalanche came down in Rogers Pass. It buried a train track. Men were sent to clear the track. They worked at night in the wind and snow.

Stop and Think:

Imagine you are one of the men. How do you feel as you clear the track? Why?

As the men worked, a second avalanche came down. It pushed a steam engine 500 metres into a creek. It tossed a snowplow on top of a shed. The avalanche buried the workers alive. It took weeks to dig out the 58 bodies. Some bodies were still standing, frozen in time.

Stop and Think:

What do you think "frozen in time" means?

Men dig out the snowplow. (March 5, 1910).

Avalanches kill about 14 people a year in Canada. An avalanche starts when a layer of snow slides down a mountain. As the snow moves, it takes more snow with it. Avalanches can move up to 200 kilometres an hour. Falling rock and ice can trigger an avalanche. People can trigger an avalanche when they ski or snowmobile.

ENVIRONMENT

People buried in an avalanche may live. They live if they are dug out fast. Very few people are alive after 35 minutes. No one is alive after two hours. The power of an avalanche can bring white death.

© BigStockPhoto/Cathy Yeulet

▶▶ Check the Facts

1. Explain how an avalanche starts, then grows. Check the passage to find the answer.

2. What is the most important idea in the passage?

   (a) Avalanches can bury towns.

   (b) Avalanches have the power to destroy and kill.

▶▶ Discussion

1. How do you know that the second avalanche in Rogers Pass came down fast and strong?

2. Nature has a lot of power. For example, heavy rains can flood streets within minutes. Describe a time when you saw the power of nature.

3. Avalanches are one kind of natural danger, or hazard. What are some other natural hazards? How can people protect themselves from these natural hazards?

Mini-Lesson: Cause and Effect

Good writers use a plan to develop their ideas. One kind of plan is cause and effect. Active readers look for the writer's plan. Knowing the plan helps readers understand the writer's ideas.

Look at the idea map below.
Answer the questions that follow.

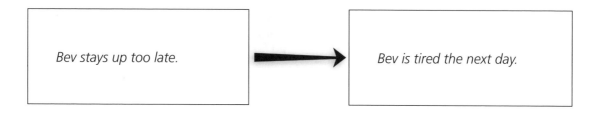

1. What happens because Bev stays up too late? _____

2. Why is Bev tired the next day? _____

The idea map above shows a connection between two ideas.
The idea in the first box is the **cause**. A cause makes something happen.
The idea in the second box is the **effect**. An effect is the thing that happens.

Look at the idea map below. Add an effect.
Say or write an idea that makes sense.

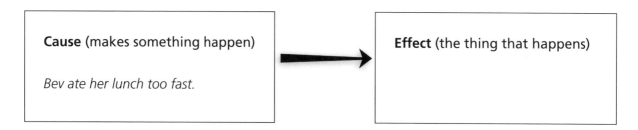

Some causes have more than one effect.

**Look at the idea map below. What is the cause?
How many effects does the cause have?**

Cause

Avalanches have the power to destroy and kill.

Effect

Avalanches can sweep trees down mountains.

Effect

Avalanches can bury towns.

Effect

Avalanches can trap people in snow.

**Read the paragraph below.
Finish the cause and effect idea map.**

A second avalanche came down. It pushed a steam engine 500 metres into a creek. It tossed a snowplow on top of a shed. The avalanche buried the workers alive.

Cause

A second avalanche came down in Rogers Pass.

Effect

It pushed a steam engine 500 metres into a creek.

Effect

Effect

It buried the workers alive.

Literacy Practice: Thermometer

Thermometers tell us the temperature.
What else do people use thermometers for?

A thermometer measures temperature in
degrees. The degrees are called Celcius degrees.
We write and read temperatures like this:

© BigStockPhoto/Aleksey Kozin

    10°C   ten degrees Celcius

    -10°C   minus ten degrees Celcius

Look at the thermometer on page 67.
Read the sentences below. Choose the correct temperature.

1. Water starts to boil at   (a) over 100°C   (b) 100°C   (c) below 100°C

2. Water starts to freeze at   (a) 10°C   (b) 0°C   (c) -10°C

3. Many people keep the temperature in their home at   (a) 19°C   (b) 21°C (c) 30°C

   How did you figure out the answer?

4. Normal body temperature is   (a) 30°C   (b) 37°C   (c) 40°C

   How did you figure out the answer?

▶▶ Discussion

5.   Look at the thermometer again.
       Is it a good day for a long bike ride?
       Give a reason for your answer.

ENVIRONMENT

Thermometer

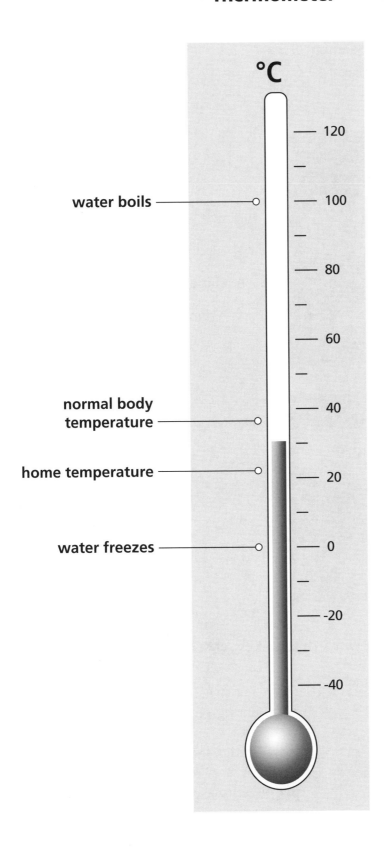

°C

water boils — 100

normal body temperature — 40

home temperature — 20

water freezes — 0

120

80

60

-20

-40

Word Attack 1: Predict the Word

Look at each picture. Finish the sentence.
Think of a word that makes sense.
Say or write your word.

1. Avalanches start in the

   _____.

2. A _____ can start an avalanche.

Finish the sentences. Think of a word that makes sense.
Say or write your word.

1. An avalanche can be _____ enough to push trains off tracks.

2. People die if they are _____ under snow for too long.

3. Some dogs can _____ people who are buried in snow.

4. We use a _____ to check the temperature.

ENVIRONMENT

Word Attack 2: Word Families

Look at the words in the box below.
Look for letter patterns.
Group the words into three word families.

The first one is an example.

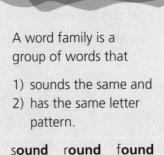

A word family is a group of words that

1) sounds the same and
2) has the same letter pattern.

sound   round   found

kill ✓	hide	will	wide
slide	ride	lock	block
rock	sock	fill	still

ill   **ide**   **ock**

kill

Read each sentence.
Circle two words that have the bolded letter pattern.

ill   1. Avalanches still kill 14 people a year in Canada.

ide   2. Avalanches cover a wide area as they slide.

ock   3. Avalanches can split rocks. They can block mountain roads.

Word Attack 3: Long Vowel Sounds

**A. Say the words. Focus on the bolded letters.
What sound do the bolded letters make?**

week   creek   sweep

clear   steam   year

bury   body   very

All the bolded letters make the long /e/ sound.

**B. Finish the sentences. Use a word that has a long /e/ sound.
Think of a word that makes sense. Say or write your word.**

1. _____ make honey.

2. My _____ hurt from standing.

3. What does this word _____ ?

4. That's dirty. Here's a _____ one.

5. Ha ha! You're so _____ .

6. She won't help. She's _____ .

Are your words in the box?
If yes, check your spelling.

funny	mean	lazy
clean	Bees	feet

**C. Read each sentence out loud. Circle
two words that have the long /e/ sound.**

/ee/ 1. The deep snow protects the trees.

/ea/ 2. The sun rises in the east. The sun's
         heat will melt the snow.

/y/   3. On a sunny day, the snow looks
         shiny.

© BigStockPhoto/Paul Yates

Environment

Tsunami!

Mini-Lesson: Cause and Effect

Literacy Practice: Map

▶▶ Discussion

Imagine you are on a beach, looking at the ocean. You see a wall of water coming at you. What do you do?

This wall of water is called a tsunami. In 2004, a tsunami hit 13 countries in Asia. A ten-year-old girl saved many people. Her name was Tilly Smith.

Read the passage on the next two pages. Learn how Tilly saved so many people.

Tsunami!

Tilly Smith was just ten years old. But she saved the lives of many people. Tilly was on holidays. She was at a beach in Thailand. The water looked white and bubbly, like the foam on beer. People on the beach did not know why. But Tilly knew. She knew a tsunami can make ocean water look like foam.

"Run!" Tilly yelled. Tilly's family ran. They warned people a tsunami was coming. People ran for their lives! They were safe. At other beaches, the tsunami killed many people.

Stop and Think:

Imagine you are one of the people on the beach. Would you listen to Tilly and run? Why or why not?

Most tsunamis are caused by an earthquake deep in the ocean. Out in the ocean, the tsunami waves may be just 30 centimetres high. But when they reach the shore, they can be 30 metres high!

Tsunami waves can move across the ocean as fast as a jet plane. Closer to shore, the waves slow down. But they still move fast. People must run for their lives to escape.

© BigStockPhoto/Manuel Ribeiro

© BigStockPhoto/Mana Photo

© Pacific Tsunami Museum

ENVIRONMENT

Tsunami waves look like walls of water. They can keep coming for hours. They wash away roads and buildings. Thousands of people can lose their homes.

Stop and Think:

How do you think Tilly learned about tsunamis?

Tilly's teacher taught the class about tsunamis. Tilly learned how to spot the danger signs. Learning about tsunamis can save lives.

Tsunamis wash away homes.

▶▶ Check the Facts

1. Explain how a tsunami starts, then grows. Check the passage to find the answer.

2. What is the most important idea in the passage?

   (a) Stay away from beaches.

   (b) Tsunamis are fast, big, and powerful.

▶▶ Discussion

1. Why do you think so many people die in tsunamis?

2. Have you ever warned someone that something bad was going to happen? Did they listen to you? Why or why not?

3. A person's true character comes out in hard times. Do you agree? Why or why not?

Mini-Lesson: Cause and Effect

Good writers use a plan to develop their ideas. One kind of plan is cause and effect. The **cause** makes something happen. The **effect** is the thing that happens.

Read the paragraphs.
Finish the cause and effect idea maps.

Paragraph 1   "Run!" Tilly yelled. Tilly's family ran. They warned people a tsunami was coming. People ran for their lives! They were safe.

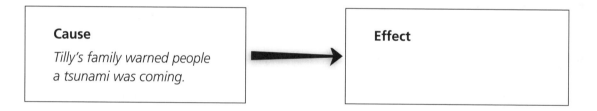

Cause

Tilly's family warned people a tsunami was coming.

Effect

Paragraph 2   Earthquakes have a lot of power. Sometimes earthquakes happen deep in the ocean. These earthquakes can cause tsunamis.

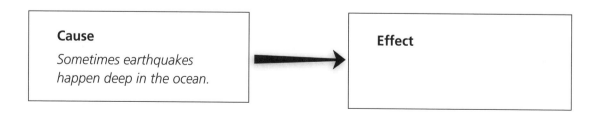

Cause

Sometimes earthquakes happen deep in the ocean.

Effect

Paragraph 3   Tsunami waves can keep coming for hours. They wash out roads and buildings. Thousands of people can lose their homes.

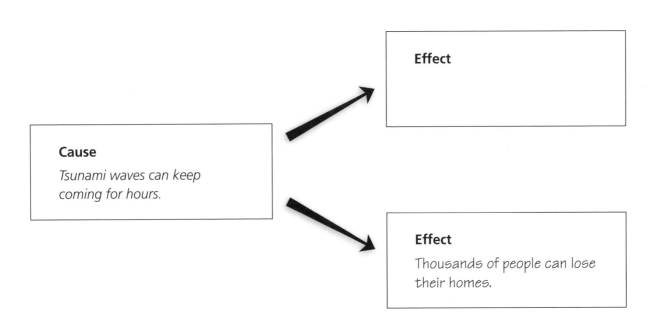

Cause

Tsunami waves can keep coming for hours.

Effect

Effect

Thousands of people can lose their homes.

Literacy Practice: Map

Some people like to read maps. Other people avoid them. The trick to reading a map is knowing the different parts.

Look at the map on page 77. Find these parts on the map:

- the title
- the key
- the compass
- the scale

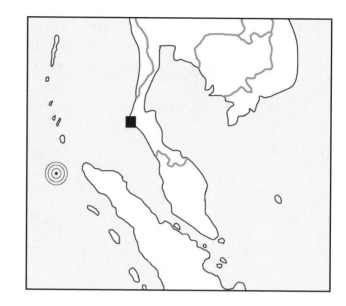

Now answer these questions:

1. What is the title of the map? Copy it here: _____

Key: The key explains the meaning of symbols on a map. For example, the symbol ★ usually means capital city.

2. How many symbols are in the map's key? _____

3. What does ◎ stand for? _____

4. What does ■ stand for? _____

5. In which country is Tilly's beach? Circle the name of the country.

Compass: A compass shows direction.

6. Look at the map. Where did the tsunami start? Circle the correct answer.

    The tsunami started (south / west / east) of Indonesia.

Scale: A scale shows distance. The scale for this map shows 1,000 kilometres.

7. About how many kilometres did the tsunami go to reach Tilly's beach?

    (a) 100   (b) 500   (c) 1,000

    How did you figure out the answer?

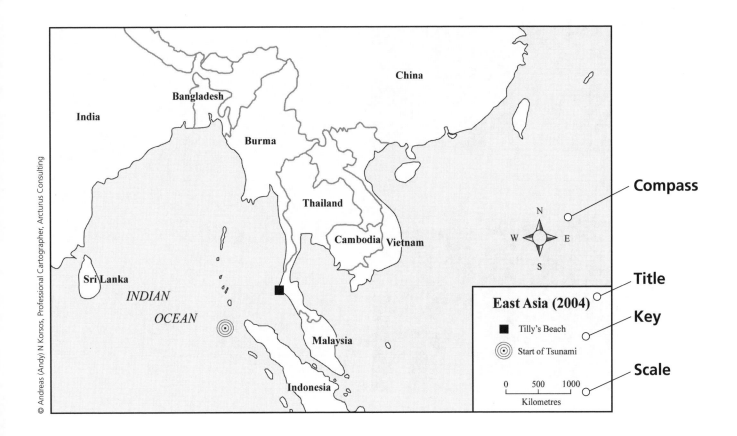

© Andreas (Andy) N Korsos, Professional Cartographer, Arcturus Consulting

Word Attack 1: Predict the Word

Look at each picture. Finish the sentence.
Think of a word that makes sense.
Say or write your word.

1. Tsunamis cause a lot of damage
   to _____.

2. A tsunami can wash away
   _____ .

Finish the sentences. Think of a word that makes sense.
Say or write your word.

1. Many _____ such as India have been hit by tsunamis.

2. Tsunamis are fast and _____.

3. In many cases, people have no _____ that a tsunami is coming.

4. People are lucky to _____ when they get caught in a tsunami.

ENVIRONMENT

Word Attack 2: Word Families

Look at the words in the box below.
Group the words into three word families.
Each word family has the same letter pattern.

The first one is an example.

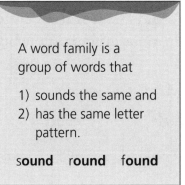

A word family is a group of words that

1) sounds the same and
2) has the same letter pattern.

sound r**ound** f**ound**

save ✓	more	boss	before
shore	loss	tore	toss
across	wave	gave	brave

ave   **ore**   **oss**

save _____   _____   _____

_____   _____   _____

_____   _____   _____

_____   _____   _____

Read each sentence.
Circle two words that have the bolded letter pattern.

ave   1. Tilly gave many people a chance to save their lives.

ore   2. I know more about tsunamis now than I did before.

oss   3. A tsunami can toss boats into the air as it moves across the ocean.

Word Attack 3: Long Vowel Sounds

A. Say the words. Focus on the bolded letters.
What sound do the bolded letters make?

wh**i**te   l**i**ke   t**i**me

h**igh**   s**igh**   f**igh**t

wh**y**   m**y**   sp**y**

All the bolded letters make the long /i/ sound.

B. Finish the sentences. Use a word that has a long /i/ sound.
Think of a word that makes sense. Say or write your word.

1. Look at the camera. _____!

2. I ride my _____ to work.

3. I draw with my _____ hand.

4. I did not sleep all _____.

5. Don't _____. It will be okay.

6. Fish swim; birds _____.

Are your words in the box?
If yes, check your spelling.

cry	fly	smile
night	bike	right

C. Read the sentences out loud. Circle two
words that have the long /i/ sound.

/i/   1. A tsunami can be miles wide.

/igh/ 2. A tsunami can drop out of sight in
          the ocean. Or it might hit land.

/y/   3. By reading about tsunamis, we
          can try to learn more about them.

History
The Beaver

Mini-Lesson: Timeline

Literacy Practice: Symbol

▶▶ Discussion

Busy as a beaver. Why do you think we use the word *busy* to describe beavers?

Beavers have lived in Canada for thousands of years. In the 1600s, white men came for the beavers. The white men came from Britain and France.

Read the passage on the next two pages. Learn why white men came for the beavers.

The Beaver

Beavers helped shape the landscape of Canada. Long ago, more beavers than people lived across this land. The beavers built dams. The dams helped to make wetlands.

Stop and Think:

Can you think of other ways that beavers have shaped the landscape?

Beavers also helped shape the history of Canada. In the 1600s, men in Europe wore felt hats. The hats were made from fur. The fur came from beaver pelts. So white men came to this land for beaver pelts.

First Nations trappers traded with the white men. The trappers traded beaver pelts for goods like pots and tools. The trappers showed the white men how to trap. They took the white men on the rivers. The white men got to know the land. Many more white people came to live here.

By the 1880s, beaver hats were no longer popular. This was good news for the beavers! The beavers were almost wiped out by trapping.

Stop and Think:

Do you think trapping beavers became easier or harder over the years?

Beaver dams help make wetlands.

First Nations trappers trade with white men.

In 1851, the beaver was put on Canada's first stamp. In 1937, the beaver was put on the nickel. In 1975, the government passed the Beaver Bill. This law named the beaver as a symbol of Canada. The hard-working beaver remains a symbol of our country today.

Canada's first stamp.

▶▶ Check the Facts

1. Explain how the beaver brought the First Nations and white people together. Check the passage to find the answer.

2. What is the most important idea in the passage?

(a) Beavers were almost wiped out by trapping.

(b) Beavers helped shape Canada's history and landscape.

▶▶ Discussion

1. Imagine that men in Europe never wore felt hats made from fur. How would Canada's history be different?

2. Do you think the beaver is a good symbol for Canada and its people? Give a reason for your answer.

3. Trapping almost wiped out the beaver. Do you think we should have laws that protect wild animals. Why or why not?

Mini-Lesson: Timeline

Good writers use a plan to develop their ideas. One kind of plan is a timeline. Writers use timelines to put ideas in the order that they happen.

Look at the timeline below.
It tells the history of the beaver.
Answer the questions that follow.

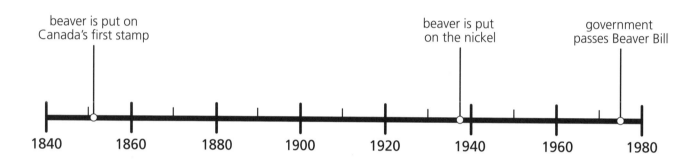

1. (a) The first two years marked on the timeline are 1840 and 1860. How many years are between these two years?

   (i) 20 years   (ii) 40 years   (iii) 60 years

   How did you figure out the answer?

   (b) Put an X on the timeline to show the year 1850.

   How did you figure out where to put the X?

2. When did the government pass the Beaver Bill? _____

   How did you figure out the answer?

3. The last year on the timeline is 1980. How many years does the timeline show in total?

   (a) 1980   (b) 160   (c) 140

   How did you figure out the answer?

Grey Owl

Grey Owl was a white man. But he told people he was First Nations. He started as a trapper. He became famous for his love of nature.

© Glenbow Archives/NA-4868-211

Look at the timeline below. It tells the history of Grey Owl. Answer the questions that follow.

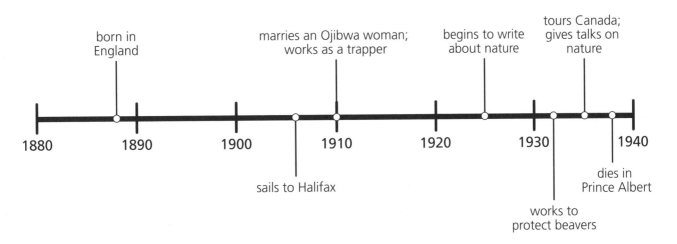

1. The first two years marked on the timeline are 1880 and 1890. Put an X on the timeline to show the year 1885.

2. When was Grey Owl born?   (a) between 1880 and 1885

   (b) between 1885 and 1890

3. What did Grey Owl do in 1935?   (a) He began to write about nature.

   (b) He gave talks about nature.

4. About how old was Grey Owl when he died?   (a) 40   (b) 50   (c) 60

   How did you figure out the answer?

Literacy Practice: Symbol

Symbols are a big part of our lives. They come in many shapes and forms. For example, the beaver is a symbol that means hard-working. A green light is a symbol that means go.

We use symbols for many reasons:

1. Symbols are easy to understand.
   What does the symbol in Box 1 mean?

2. Symbols are easy to read. In some cases, different symbols can mean the same thing. What do all the symbols in Box 2 mean?

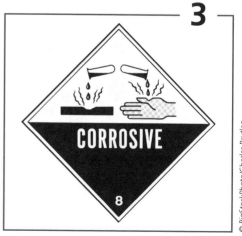

3. Symbols can say a lot in a simple way. What does the symbol in Box 3 say?

Look at the symbols below.
What do you think they mean?
Compare your ideas with the Answer Key.

What symbols do you see in your daily life?

Word Attack 1: Predict the Word

Look at each picture. Finish the sentence.
Think of a word that makes sense.
Say or write your word.

> What do you do if you can't read a word?
>
> Active readers think of a word that makes sense.

1. This man traps _____.

2. This _____ is pretty.

Finish the sentences. Think of a word that makes sense.
Say or write your word.

1. A green _____ is a symbol. It means go.

2. A beaver cuts down trees and builds _____.

3. The _____ passed the Beaver Bill in 1975.

4. A penny is one cent. A _____ is five cents.

HISTORY

Word Attack 2: Word Families

Look at the words in the box below.
Group the words into three word families.
Each word family has the same letter pattern.

The first one is an example.

> A word family is a
> group of words that
>
> 1) sounds the same and
> 2) has the same letter
>   pattern.
>
> **sound   round   found**

land ✓	seed	feed	weed
about	sand	hand	snout
need	shout	pout	stand

and   **out**   **eed**

_____land_____   _____   _____

_____   _____   _____

_____   _____   _____

_____   _____   _____

Read the sentences.
Circle two words that have the bolded letter pattern.

and   1. Beavers work hard on land. They use their claws
          to dig up stones, sand, and mud.

out   2. Beavers are about one metre long from their snout
          to the end of their tail.

eed   3. Beavers need trees. They feed on leaves, buds, and bark.

Word Attack 3: Long Vowel Sounds

**A. Say the words. Focus on the bolded letters.
What sound do the bolded letters make?**

cl**o**se   b**o**ne   n**o**te

sh**ow**   fl**ow**   mead**ow**

r**oa**d   f**oa**m   l**oa**d

All the bolded letters make the long /o/ sound.

**B. Finish the sentences. Use a word that has a long /o/ sound.
Think of a word that makes sense. Say or write your word.**

1. Wipe your runny _____.

2. What a funny _____!

3. _____ out the candles.

4. Put it higher. It's too _____.

5. The fishing _____ sank.

6. _____ the stain in water.

Are your words in the box?
If yes, check your spelling.

blow	nose	low
boat	soak	joke

**C. Read the sentences out loud. Circle two
words that have the long /o/ sound.**

/o/   1. Beavers build homes in the deep
          open water of ponds.

/oa/   2. Beavers dig canals to float logs to the
          pond. They use the canals like roads.

/ow/   3. A beaver's front teeth never stop
          growing. Did you know that?

© BigStockPhoto/Michel Loiselle

HISTORY

© BigStockPhoto/Chiya Li

History
The Maple Leaf

Mini-Lesson: Timeline

Literacy Practice: Menu

© BigStockPhoto/Edite Artmann

▶▶ Discussion

The maple leaf is a symbol of Canada. It is on Canada's flag. Where else do you see this symbol?

Read the passage on the next two pages. Learn why the maple leaf is one of Canada's symbols.

The Maple Leaf

The maple tree is a big part of our history. First Nations people used sap from the maple tree. They cooked the sap to make syrup. They gave thanks to the maple tree.

Making maple syrup.

In the 1600s, people from France came to this land. These white people had to learn new things. First Nations people showed them how to make syrup. The white people also made maple sugar.

Stop and Think:

How is the maple tree a part of your life?

In 1858, the maple leaf was put on silver coins. Soon, all coins had a maple leaf. The maple leaf is still on the penny. The mayor of Montreal talked about the maple leaf. He said the maple leaf was the king of the forest.

Stop and Think:

Why do you think the mayor said the maple was the "king of the forest"?

In 1867, Canada became a nation. A group in Montreal held a poetry contest. People wrote poems about Canada. Today, no one knows who won the contest. But we know which poem came in second. The poem is now the song "The Maple Leaf Forever." This song was a hit for many years.

In 1964, Canada wanted to choose a flag. Many people sent in designs. Many designs had a maple leaf. Now the maple leaf is on our flag. The maple leaf is a symbol of Canada.

© BigStockPHoto/Chiya Li

▶▶ Check the Facts

1. Find three examples that show the maple tree is a big part of Canada's history. Check the passage to find the answer.

2. What is the most important idea in the passage?

(a) The maple leaf has a long history in Canada.

(b) The maple leaf is on Canada's flag.

▶▶ Discussion

1. Why do you think the First Nations people gave thanks to the maple tree?

2. Do you think the maple leaf is a good symbol for Canada and its people? Give a reason for your answer.

3. The maple leaf is on the back of the penny. What is on the back of other Canadian coins? What do you know about these symbols of Canada? How can you find out more?

Mini-Lesson: Timeline

Writers use timelines to put ideas in the order that they happen.

Look at the timeline below.
It tells the history of the maple leaf.
Answer the questions that follow.

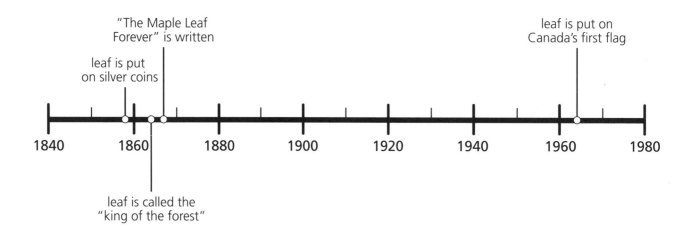

1. Find the years 1840 and 1860 on the timeline. Put an X on the timeline to show the year 1850. How did you figure out the answer?

2. When was the maple leaf put on silver coins?

    (a) between 1840 and 1850   (b) between 1850 and 1860

3. When was the maple leaf put on Canada's flag?

    (a) between 1960 and 1965   (b) between 1965 and 1970

    How did you figure out the answer?

4. The maple leaf was put on coins in 1858. How many years passed before the maple leaf was put on Canada's flag?

    (a) less than a hundred years   (b) more than a hundred years

Canada Becomes a Nation

Canada became a nation in 1867.
Only four provinces were a part of
Canada at that time—Ontario, Quebec,
Nova Scotia, and New Brunswick.
The timeline below shows when every
province and territory joined Canada.

Look at the timeline.
Answer the questions that follow.

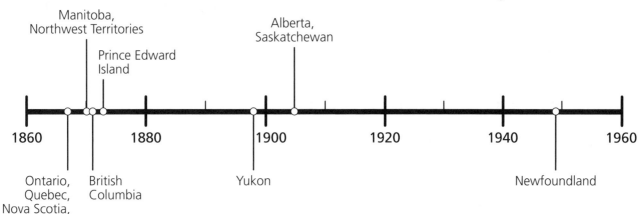

1. When did Canada grow more?   (a) 1860 to 1880   (b) 1880 to 1920

2. Put an X on the timeline to show the year 1910.

3. When did Alberta and Saskatchewan join Canada? (a) 1902   (b) 1905   (c) 1909

   How did you figure out the answer?

4. (a) When did the Yukon join Canada?   (i) 1890   (ii) 1898   (iii) 1902

   (b) When did Newfoundland join Canada?   (i) 1945   (ii) 1949   (iii) 1959

   (c) About how many years after the Yukon did Newfoundland join Canada?

      (i) 30   (ii) 50   (iii) 70

      How did you figure out the answer?

Literacy Practice: Menu

Menus are organized in different ways. For example, menus can be organized by types of food such as soups and salads. Or menus can be organized by meals: breakfast, lunch, and dinner.

Look at the menu on page 97.
The menu is for a restaurant called
The Pancake House.

Answer these questions:

1. Which meal is shown on the menu?   (a) breakfast   (b) lunch   (c) dinner

2. The breakfast meals are listed in two groups.

   (a) How many meals are listed under Breakfast Specials? _____

   (b) How much do Breakfast Specials cost? _____

   (c) What food is in both meals under Breakfast Specials? _____

3. What is the most expensive drink on the menu? _____

▶▶ Discussion

4. Why are Breakfast Favourites so expensive?

5. Which meal is cheaper?   (a) Buttermilk Pancakes and tea

   (b) the House Breakfast

   Which meal would you order, (a) or (b)? Why?

6. You take your two kids to The Pancake House. You have a gift certificate for $20.00. What food and drinks would you order for the three of you?

The Pancake House

Breakfast Specials $5.99

Strawberry Pancakes
Two pancakes served with fresh berries. Topped with whipped cream.

Buttermilk Pancakes
Three pancakes served with lots of maple syrup. Just like Mom makes!

Breakfast Favourites
(Tea and coffee included)

Country Breakfast	**$11.99**

Bacon and ham served with 3 eggs and 3 berry pancakes.

Big Boy Breakfast	**$14.99**

Bacon, sausage and ham served with 3 eggs, 5 berry pancakes and toast.

Drinks

Milk	$1.75
Juice	$2.25
Hot Chocolate	$2.50
Coffee or Tea	$1.25

House Breakfast $8.50

A stack of 5 buttermilk pancakes served with 2 sausages.

(All the coffee you can drink!)

Word Attack 1: Predict the Word

Look at each picture. Finish the sentence.
Think of a word that makes sense.
Say or write your word.

1. The sap drips into a

   _____ .

2. Maple syrup comes in

   _____ .

Finish the sentences. Think of a word that makes sense.
Say or write your word.

1. Maple wood is used to make _____ like tables and chairs.

2. Nickels and dimes are examples of Canadian _____ .

3. Canada has ten provinces and three _____ .

4. The beaver and maple leaf are _____ of Canada.

HISTORY

Word Attack 2: Word Families

Look at the words in the box below.
Group the words into three word families.
Each word family has the same letter pattern.

The first one is an example.

A word family is a
group of words that

1) sounds the same and
2) has the same letter
   pattern.

sound **round** **found**

year ✓	rent	went	hear
song	near	strong	wrong
sent	long	spent	clear

ear	**ong**	**ent**
year		

Read the sentences.
Circle two words that have the bolded pattern.

ear   1. It is the year 1880 in Quebec City. People hear "O Canada"
           for the first time.

ong   2. The song says that Canada is a strong and free country.

ent   3. Writers spent a lot of time on the words for "O Canada." The
           song went through many changes over the years.

Word Attack 3: Long Vowel Sounds

A. Say the words. Focus on the bolded letters.
All the bolded letters make one of the /u/ sounds.

grew	few	threw
soon	moose	food
rule	cube	tune

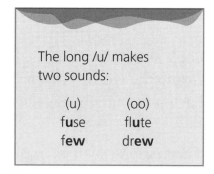

The long /u/ makes two sounds:

(u)	(oo)
fuse	flute
few	drew

B. Finish the sentences. Use a word that has a long /u/ sound.
Think of a word that makes sense. Say or write your word.

1. That's old. Give me a_____one.

2. _____ your food. Then swallow.

3. She dove into the_____.

4. Tie it tighter. It's too_____.

5. _____ comes before July.

6. What a_____baby!

Are your words in the box?
If yes, check your spelling.

cute	loose	new
Chew	June	pool

C. Read the sentences out loud. Circle two
words that have a long /u/ sound.

/ew/ 1. The maple leaf flew. We knew the flag was Canada's.

/oo/ 2. The flag was red and white. That, too, was proof it was Canada's flag.

/u/ 3. We use the flag with respect. It is a huge part of our history.

© BigStockPhoto/Chiya Li

In some cases, the answer key contains only a few of the possible responses for questions. There are other acceptable responses for these questions.

People

Unit 1: Clara Hughes

Check the Facts: 1. Clara wanted to speed skate for Canada. She won gold and bronze medals in the Olympics. Clara wanted to help children. She works with groups that help children play sports. **2.** a
Discussion: 1. Possible responses: children who do not have a lot of chances in life; children who always get into trouble; children who lack self-confidence; children who do not have positive role models **2.** Student responses will vary. **3.** Student responses will vary.

Mini-Lesson: (p. 5) Possible responses: **Top Chart: 1. Inference:** I think he is hot. **Why:** I know that people sweat when they are hot. **2. Inference:** I think it was autumn (fall). **Why:** I know that leaves fall off the trees in autumn. **Bottom Chart: Inference:** I think Clara is a great athlete. **Why:** I know that only the best athletes can win gold at the Olympics.

Literacy Practice: 1a. iii **1b.** i **1c.** ii **2a.** Crime Stop **2b.** 10:00 **3a.** 11 and 22 **3b.** 2 and 6 **4.** Watch it on channel 24. **5.** Student responses will vary.

Predict the Word: 1. children **2.** Cycling; Biking **1.** see; watch **2.** medal; game; event; race **3.** countries; places; cities; regions **4.** Training; Practising; Exercising; Coaching

Word Families: 1. pain; gain **2.** Games; name **3.** fast; past

Digraphs: Exercise B*: 1. short **2.** shoes **3.** Thank **4.** breath **5.** wrong **6.** wrist **Exercise C: 1.** shaped; should **2.** things; athlete **3.** writer; written

Unit 2: Alex Bilodeau

Check the Facts: 1. Alex came in 11th in the 2006 Games. He won a gold medal in the 2010 Games. **2.** b
Discussion: **1.** Possible responses: encourages; gives him the desire or will; makes him want (to train hard) **2.** Student responses will vary. **3.** Student responses will vary.

Mini-Lesson: (p. 14) Possible responses: **1. Inference:** I think Alex is a person who never gives up. **Why:** I know that many people would give up after finishing 11th. But Alex did not give up. He trained harder. **2. Inference:** I think Alex is very athletic. **Why:** I know that learning to ski is hard. Jumping, flipping, and twisting in the air is even harder. **(p. 15)** Possible responses: **Paragraph 1:** I think Frederic is a fighter. I think Frederic has a positive attitude. I think Frederic is a person who never gives up. **Paragraph 2:** I think Frederic likes to take risks. I think Frederic likes excitement. I think Frederic likes to help people.

Literacy Practice: (p. 17) 1a. ii **1b.** ii **2a.** i **2b.** iii **3.** Noon–3:00 p.m. **4.** T **5a.** no **5b.** 6 **5c.** 2:30 p.m.–7:30 p.m. **5d.** iii **5e.** 22 **6.** Student responses will vary.

Predict the Word: 1. difficult; dangerous; hard **2.** cheered; screamed; yelled **1.** people; children **2.** skiing; skating; snowboarding; snowmobiling **3.** baseball; football; golf **4.** strong; fit; active; healthy

Word Families: 1. rang; bang **2.** hate; late **3.** jump; dump

Digraphs: Exercise B: 1. change **2.** chips **3.** stuck **4.** stick **5.** Where **6.** Which **Exercise C: 1.** choose; changes **2.** lucky; backs **3.** while; whips

Relationships

Unit 3: The List

Check the Facts: 1. First Visit: Anna forgets to tell the doctor everything. Anna feels upset after the visit. Anna does not have a list. **Second Visit:** Anna remembers to tell the doctor everything. Anna feels happy after the visit. Anna has a list. **2.** b **Discussion: 1.** Possible responses: Anna tells her friend everything about her health. Anna phones her friend when she feels upset. Anna's friend takes time to help Anna write a list. **2.** Student responses will vary. **3.** Student responses will vary.

Mini-Lesson: (p. 24) 1. a, c **2.** a, b **3.** a, c **(p. 25) 1.** a, b **2.** a, c **3.** a, c **4.** b, c **5.** a, b

Literacy Practice: 1. F **2.** F **3.** T **4.** F **5.** T **6.** T **7.** No. Visit the doctor if the sore throat does not go away after seven days.

Predict the Word: 1. writes; makes; prints; prepares **2.** headache; migraine **1.** medical; health; serious; personal **2.** stomach **3.** allergic; sensitive **4.** bruise; mark; spot

Word Families: 1. think; pink **2.** shake; take **3.** best; test

Blends: Exercise B: 1. slam **2.** Slow **3.** smart **4.** smell **5.** trust **6.** trees **Exercise C: 1.** Slurp; Slice **2.** small; smoothie **3.** trick; try

Unit 4: The Phone Call

Check the Facts: 1. Jenny learns there are people who help tenants. She learns she has legal rights. She learns landlords must fix things. She learns she should write a letter to the landlord. She learns to be firm with her landlord. **2.** b **Discussion: 1.** Possible responses: The landlord feels Jenny does not know her rights, so he does not worry about fixing the stove. Jenny was not firm enough in her first phone message, so the landlord thinks Jenny is not too worried about her stove. The landlord is very busy or very lazy. **2.** Student responses will vary. **3.** Student responses will vary.

Mini-Lesson: (p. 34) 1. a, c **2.** b, c **3.** a, b **4.** a, c **(p. 35) Paragraph 1:** It is too small. The tenants next door are noisy. **Paragraph 2:** The police told Sal his car was stolen. He slipped and broke his leg.

. . . . (102) . . . .

THE ACTIVE READER

Literacy Practice: 2. e **3.** g **4.** a, f **5.** c **6.** f **7.** d **8.** h **9.** Student responses will vary. **10.** Pen. It is harder for someone to make changes to your cheque. **11.** No. Someone can then write in any amount and cash the cheque.

Predict the Word: 1. building; apartment; walk-up **2.** information; paperwork; rules; documents
1. message **2.** landlord **3.** daycare; playschool; kindergarten; friend's; relative's **4.** colour

Word Families: 1. back; crack **2.** trace; place **3.** tell; well

Blends: Exercise B: 1. plan **2.** plus **3.** glad **4.** gloves **5.** Friday **6.** fresh **Exercise C: 1.** plumber; plugged **2.** glue; glass **3.** from; freezing

Health and Safety

Unit 5: The Burn

Check the Facts: 1. John runs his hand under cold water for 15 minutes. He lets the air dry his burned fingers. Mina washes her hands before helping John. Mina gently tapes a clean cloth over the burn. **2.** a
Discussion: 1. Possible responses: **John:** careless or clumsy—he often burns his fingers; a good father—he cooks meals for his daughter. **Mina:** mature—She knows how to treat a burn; funny—She makes a joke about sending her father a bill. **2.** Student responses will vary. **3.** Student responses will vary.

Mini-Lesson: (p. 44) How to Make a Cup of Tea: 2, 3, 1, 4 **Word Clues:** First, While (the water heats up), Then, Finally **How to Treat a Burn:** 4, 1, 3, 2 **Word Clues:** Then, When (the burn is dry), Finally
(p. 45) 1. c **2.** First, Next, Then, When (enough aloe oozes out)

Literacy Practice: 1. Types of Burns **2a.** Second-degree **2b.** Third-degree **3a.** How the burn looks and feels **3b.** How to treat the burn **4a.** T **4b.** F **4c.** F **4d.** T **5.** A second-degree burn is redder. It swells more. It hurts more. It forms a blister.

Predict the Word: 1. dishcloth; dishtowel; cloth; towel **2.** blister **1.** fingers **2.** careful **3.** swells; hurts; stings **4.** emergency

Word Families: 1. prick; stick **2.** Bring; thing **3.** shape; tape

Blends: Exercise B: 1. Stand **2.** stars **3.** grow **4.** grass **5.** blanket **6.** blind **Exercise C: 1.** first; sting **2.** degree; great **3.** bleed; black

Unit 6: Medicine

Check the Facts: 1. Carla goes to the doctor and gets a prescription. She goes to the drugstore to get the prescription filled. She reads the label on the medicine bottle. She phones the pharmacist to ask questions. She gives Tony the medicine until it is all gone. **2.** b **Discussion: 1.** Possible responses: The pharmacist tells Carla to give the medicine to Tony until it is all gone. The medicine label says to give the medicine until it is gone. Taking all the medicine kills all the germs or viruses. If Tony does not get all the medicine, he might get sick again. **2.** Student responses will vary. **3.** Possible responses: **Side Effects:** feeling dizzy, feeling sleepy, getting a rash, stomach upset, fever **Visit a Doctor:** People should see a doctor if the side effects are severe or not listed on the information sheet.

Mini-Lesson: (p. 54) Carla's Story: 2, 5, 3, 1, 4 **Word Clues:** First, After (Carla got home), Then, After (seven days), Finally **Becky's Fever:** 4, 2, 1, 3 **Word Clues:** First, Then, While (on the phone), The next day **(p. 55) Word Clues:** First, Then, After (talking to his friends), Finally **Sequence:** 4, 1, 3, 5, 2

Literacy Practice: 2. c **3.** c **4.** g **5.** f **6.** d **7.** a **8.** e **9.** b **10.** Check the name of who the prescription is for. Check the doctor's name. Check the drug name (if you know it).

Predict the Word: 1. pharmacist; woman **2.** syringe **1.** drugstore; pharmacy **2.** label; information **3.** tissue; Kleenex **4.** temperature

Word Families: 1. must; just **2.** light; night **3.** told; hold

Long Vowel Sounds: Exercise B: 1. safe **2.** game **3.** drain **4.** jail **5.** say **6.** crayons **Exercise C: 1.** label; take **2.** wait; pain **3.** away; day

Environment

Unit 7: Avalanche!

Check the Facts: 1. An avalanche starts in the mountains. It is triggered by something such as falling rock or ice. A layer of snow starts to slide down the mountain. The layer of snow takes more snow with it as it goes down the mountain. The avalanche gets bigger and bigger. **2.** b **Discussion: 1.** The avalanche was so fast that the men were buried as they worked. They did not have time to get away. The avalanche was strong enough to move a steam engine and a snowplow. **2.** Student responses will vary. **3.** Possible responses: flooding, lightning strike, mudslide, tsunami, blizzard, hurricane, tornado, heat wave

Mini-Lesson: (p. 65) Effect: It tossed a snowplow on top of a shed.

Literacy Practice: 1. b **2.** b **3.** b **4.** b **5.** Possible responses: No. It is too hot. You might get heatstroke or sunstroke. Yes. But you should take a lot of breaks, drink a lot of water, and wear clothes that protect you from the sun.

Predict the Word: 1. mountains **2.** snowmobile; snowmobiler; Ski-Doo **1.** strong; powerful **2.** trapped; buried; stuck; covered **3.** rescue; save; find; smell **4.** thermometer

Word Families: 1. still; kill **2.** wide; slide **3.** rocks; block

Long Vowel Sounds: Exercise B: 1. Bees **2.** feet **3.** mean **4.** clean **5.** funny **6.** lazy **Exercise C: 1.** deep; trees **2.** heat; disappear **3.** sunny; shiny

Unit 8: Tsunami!

Check the Facts: 1. An earthquake happens under the ocean. Waves form in the ocean. At first, the waves are small. But they get bigger, higher, and faster as they move across the ocean. **2.** b
Discussion: 1. Possible responses: Tsunamis move so fast that people do not have time to run away. Tsunamis smash people against buildings and trees. People drown because the water is moving so fast. People do not know the signs that show a tsunami is coming. **2.** Student responses will vary. **3.** Student responses will vary.

Mini-Lesson: Paragraph 1: Effect: The people ran and were safe. **Paragraph 2: Effect:** These earthquakes can cause tsunamis. **Paragraph 3: Effect:** They wash out roads and buildings.

Literacy Practice: 1. East Asia (2004) **2.** 2 **3.** start of tsunami **4.** Tilly's beach **5.** Thailand **6.** west
7. c

Predict the Word: 1. houses; homes; buildings **2.** parking lots **1.** countries; places **2.** powerful; strong; dangerous **3.** warning; sign; idea **4.** survive; live; escape

Word Families: 1. gave; save **2.** more; before **3.** toss; across

Long Vowel Sounds: Exercise B: 1. Smile **2.** bike **3.** right **4.** night **5.** cry **6.** fly **Exercise C: 1.** miles; wide **2.** sight; might **3.** By; try

History

Unit 9: The Beaver

Check the Facts: 1. The First Nations people gave the white men beaver pelts, and the white men gave the First Nations people different kinds of goods. The First Nations people showed the white men how to trap beavers. **2.** b **Discussion: 1.** Possible responses: The population of white people in Canada would have grown more slowly. There would have been less contact between the First Nations people and the white people. **2.** Student responses will vary. **3.** Student responses will vary.

Mini-Lesson: (p. 84) 1a. i **1b.** The X should be placed on the midway marker between the years 1840 and 1860. **2.** 1975 **3.** c **(p. 85) 1.** The X should be placed at the midway point between the years 1880 and 1890. **2.** b **3.** b **4.** b

Literacy Practice: (p. 86) 1. pirates; danger; beware **2.** washrooms; restrooms; men's and women's toilets **3.** Careful. This liquid will burn, hurt, or sting your skin. **(p. 87) 1. heart:** love; broken heart; loss of a loved one **2. X:** mistake; this is the spot; a person's mark or signature **3. road sign:** Beware of rock slides when it rains! **4. butterfly:** beauty; spring; happiness; rebirth; change

Predict the Word: 1. beavers; animals **2.** butterfly; insect **1.** light **2.** dams; shelters; homes
3. government **4.** nickel

Word Families: 1. land; sand **2.** about; snout **3.** need; feed

Long Vowel Sounds: Exercise B: 1. nose **2.** joke **3.** Blow **4.** low **5.** boat **6.** Soak **Exercise C: 1.** homes; open **2.** float; roads **3.** growing; know

Unit 10: The Maple Leaf

Check the Facts: 1. The First Nations people used the maple tree to make syrup. The white people used the maple to make sugar and syrup. The maple tree brought the white people into contact with the First Nations. The maple tree was called the "king of the forest." It became a symbol of Canada. **2.** a **Discussion: 1.** Possible response: They respected the maple tree. They used the maple tree in their daily lives. **2.** Student responses will vary. **3.** Student responses will vary.

Mini-Lesson: (p.94) 1. The X should be placed on the midway marker between the years 1840 and 1860. **2.** b **3.** a **4.** b **(p.95) 1.** a **2.** The X should be placed on the midway marker between the years 1900 and 1920. **3.** b **4a.** ii **4b.** ii **4c.** ii

Literacy Practice: 1. a **2a.** 2 **2b.** $5.99 **2c.** pancakes **3.** hot chocolate **4.** The meals are big with lots of meat. **5.** a **6.** Student responses will vary.

Predict the Word: 1. bucket; pail **2.** bottles **1.** furniture **2.** coins; money; change **3.** territories **4.** symbols

Word Families: 1. year; hear **2.** song; strong **3.** spent; went

Long Vowel Sounds: Exercise B: 1. new **2.** Chew **3.** pool **4.** loose **5.** June **6.** cute **Exercise C: 1.** flew; knew **2.** too; proof **3.** use; huge

Fleming College

Cobourg Campus
The Fleming Building, Top Floor
1005 Elgin Street West
Cobourg, ON K9A 5J4